W9-DHG-585

SAUDI ARABIA

BY GOLRIZ GOLKAR

BLASTOFF! DISCOVERY

BELLWETHER MEDIA • MINNEAPOLIS, MN

Blastoff! Discovery launches a new mission: reading to learn. Filled with facts and features, each book offers you an exciting new world to explore!

BLASTOFF! UNIVERSE

BLASTOFF! Beginners — GRADE K

BLASTOFF! READERS — GRADES 1-3

BLASTOFF! DISCOVERY — GRADE 4

This edition first published in 2021 by Bellwether Media, Inc.

No part of this publication may be reproduced in whole or in part without written permission of the publisher.
For information regarding permission, write to Bellwether Media, Inc.,
Attention: Permissions Department,
6012 Blue Circle Drive, Minnetonka, MN 55343.

Library of Congress Cataloging-in-Publication Data

Names: Golkar, Golriz, author.
Title: Saudi Arabia / by Golriz Golkar.
Other titles: Blastoff! discovery. Country profiles.
Description: Minneapolis, MN : Bellwether Media, Inc., 2021. |
    Series: Blastoff Discovery : country profiles | Includes
    bibliographical references and index. | Audience: Ages 7-13 |
    Audience: Grades 4-6 | Summary: "Engaging images accompany
    information about Saudi Arabia. The combination of high-interest
    subject matter and narrative text is intended for students in grades
    3 through 8"– Provided by publisher.
Identifiers: LCCN 2020001621 (print) | LCCN 2020001622 (ebook)
    | ISBN 9781644872574 (library binding) | ISBN
    9781681037202 (ebook)
Subjects: LCSH: Saudi Arabia–Juvenile literature. | Saudi Arabia–
    Social life and customs–Juvenile literature.
Classification: LCC DS204.25 .G65 2021 (print) | LCC DS204.25
    (ebook) | DDC 953.8–dc23
LC record available at https://lccn.loc.gov/2020001621
LC ebook record available at https://lccn.loc.gov/2020001622

Editor: Kieran Downs   Designer: Brittany McIntosh

Printed in the United States of America, North Mankato, MN.

TABLE OF CONTENTS

A CITY RISING FROM THE SANDS	4
LOCATION	6
LANDSCAPE AND CLIMATE	8
WILDLIFE	10
PEOPLE	12
COMMUNITIES	14
CUSTOMS	16
SCHOOL AND WORK	18
PLAY	20
FOOD	22
CELEBRATIONS	24
TIMELINE	26
SAUDI ARABIA FACTS	28
GLOSSARY	30
TO LEARN MORE	31
INDEX	32

A CITY RISING FROM THE SANDS

KINGDOM CENTRE TOWER - - - - - - - - -
RIYADH

A family admires the exhibits at the National Museum in Riyadh. Colorful pottery and fine **Arabic** writing show Saudi Arabia's rich history. After their visit, they take a stroll in King Abdullah Malaz Park. The park's dancing fountain splashes in the background.

PACK YOUR BAGS!

In 2019, Saudi Arabia launched a new program allowing tourists from outside of the country to visit for the first time in history.

OTHER TOP SITES

AL MASMAK FORTRESS

ASIR NATIONAL PARK

MADA'IN SALEH

PROPHET'S MOSQUE

After dinner, they stop at the Kingdom Centre Tower. Standing 984 feet (300 meters) tall, this building is one of Saudi Arabia's tallest. The skyscraper offers a breathtaking view. The desert sunset casts an orange glow over the city. The mix of ancient treasures and modern wonders makes Saudi Arabia a desert paradise!

IRAQ

JORDAN

KUWAIT

GULF OF
AQABA

MEDINA

RIYADH

SAUDI
ARABIA

JEDDAH

MECCA

RED SEA

YEMEN

PERSIAN
GULF

- - - QATAR

UNITED ARAB
EMIRATES

OMAN

Saudi Arabia is located in the **Middle East**. The country's 830,000 square miles (2,149,690 square kilometers) stretch across most of the Arabian **Peninsula**. The capital, Riyadh, is located in the center of the country.

Saudi Arabia shares borders with Jordan, Iraq, and Kuwait to the north. The waters of the Persian **Gulf** make up part of the eastern border. Saudi Arabia's eastern land neighbors are Qatar, the United Arab Emirates, and Oman. Yemen lies on the southern border. Saudi Arabia's western border lies along the waters of the Red Sea and the Gulf of Aqaba.

N
W ⊕ E
S

LANDSCAPE AND CLIMATE

A large **plateau** and the Arabian Desert cover most of Saudi Arabia. The desert of Al-Nafūd lies in the north. The sands sweep into the rocky Najd Plateau that covers the center of the country. Mount Sawdā sits among mountains that span the southwest. Coastal **plains** lie along the Red Sea.

MOUNT SAWDĀ

= ARABIAN DESERT   = NAJD PLATEAU
= RUB AL-KHALI DESERT

RUB AL-KHALI DESERT

WATER IN THE DESERT

There are no permanent rivers in Saudi Arabia. Dry riverbeds called *wadis* fill up with water when it rains. Water is also drilled from underground rock.

RIYADH

Average seasonal highs and lows

JANUARY
HIGH: 68 °F (20 °C)
LOW: 48 °F (9 °C)

APRIL
HIGH: 93 °F (34 °C)
LOW: 70 °F (21 °C)

JULY
HIGH: 111 °F (44 °C)
LOW: 84 °F (29 °C)

OCTOBER
HIGH: 95 °F (35 °C)
LOW: 70 °F (21 °C)

°F = degrees Fahrenheit
°C = degrees Celsius

Saudi Arabia has a dry climate. Temperatures are much higher during the day. Winters are cool, with snow in the southern region. Summers are extremely hot. Most rainfall occurs along the western coast. Some areas, like the Rub al-Khali Desert, can go years without rain.

WILDLIFE

Saudi Arabia's desert sands are home to many animals. Striped hyenas, Arabian wolves, and red foxes roam the landscape. Hamadryas baboons munch on fruits in their cliff-side homes. Puff adders slither through the sands. Lizards hide from the desert sun. Peregrine falcons and black kites soar in the skies.

Sea life fills the waters surrounding the country. Fish such as the flathead mullet make their homes in these waters. Dolphins and great white sharks swim in the Red Sea. Humpback whales can be found in the Persian Gulf.

ARABIAN WOLF

FLATHEAD MULLETS

PEREGRINE FALCON

ARABIAN CAMELS

Arabian camels only have one hump. That hump is mostly made up of fat. The camels can break down that fat into water and energy!

HAMADRYAS
BABOON

HAMADRYAS
BABOON
Life Span: up to 20 years
Red List Status: least concern

hamadryas baboon range =

LEAST CONCERN	NEAR THREATENED	VULNERABLE	ENDANGERED	CRITICALLY ENDANGERED	EXTINCT IN THE WILD	EXTINCT

Saudi Arabia is home to over 34 million people. Nine out of ten Saudis are of Arab origin. Some are **native** Saudis. Others come from other Arab countries such as Syria, Yemen, or Iraq. Afro-Asians are another major **ethnic** group.

The entire native population of Saudi Arabia is Muslim. Most Saudis are Sunni Muslim. Other Saudis belong to the Shi'a branch of Islam. There are people living in Saudi Arabia that are not Muslim. However, the government does not allow them to show their religion in public. Arabic is the official language of Saudi Arabia. English is also widely spoken.

FAMOUS FACE

Name: Fahad Albutairi
Birthday: May 12, 1985
Hometown: Al Khobar, Saudi Arabia
Famous for: The first professional comedian to perform on stage in Saudi Arabia and creator of one of the most popular Saudi Arabian YouTube channels

SPEAK ARABIC

MECCA

Arabic uses script instead of letters. However, Arabic words can be written with the English alphabet so you can read them.

ENGLISH	ARABIC	HOW TO SAY IT
hello	marhaban	mar-HAB-ah
goodbye	ma'a as-salama	ma ahs-sah-LAH-mah
please (to males)	min fadlak	min FAHD-lehck
please (to females)	min fadlik	min FAHD-lick
thank you	shukran	SHUH-krahn
yes	na'am	NAHM
no	laa	LAH-ah

COMMUNITIES

Most Saudis live in **urban** areas such as Riyadh or Jeddah. People in these areas often live in townhomes and apartments. Wealthy Saudis may live in palaces. City residents may travel by bus or by car. Some **rural** Saudis live in areas without running water or electricity. The **nomadic** Bedouin people travel the desert with their livestock.

JEDDAH

BEDOUIN

Many Saudi families are very big. After a couple marries, both of their families spend time together at social events. Men have a religious responsibility to take care of their families.

WOMEN WEARING *ABAYAHS* AND *HIJABS*

Saudis follow many religious customs. Both men and women must dress modestly. Men wear a **traditional** headscarf. Women must be fully covered in public. They wear a long robe known as an *abayah* to cover their bodies. A *hijab* covers their heads while a *niqab* veils their faces.

16

Saudi Arabia has strict laws regarding behavior. Men and women generally do not mix in public, even at family weddings. Many public places separate women and children from men. Women often need the permission of a male family member when making important decisions.

WOMEN'S RIGHTS

In 2019, several Saudi laws were changed to grant women more freedom. Women may now get family documents from the government and travel without a male guardian's permission. Women must also be treated equally at work.

Children attend primary school for six years. Boys and girls are put in separate classes starting in third grade. Students attend middle school for three years. They then attend three years of high school. They can choose between a general, **vocational**, or religious education.

More than half of all Saudis have **service jobs**. Sales, **tourism**, and government jobs are common. Some Saudis work in the oil industry. Oil is the country's biggest **export**. A small number of Saudis work in agriculture. They may grow crops such as wheat or dates.

OIL WORKERS

TOURISM

SOCCER

The most popular sport in Saudi Arabia is soccer. Horse and camel races also attract large crowds. Popular water sports include scuba diving, sailing, and windsurfing in the resort areas near the coasts. Women are largely discouraged from playing sports. However, some play volleyball and basketball.

CAMEL RACING

Young Saudis like to use the Internet in their free time. Video games are also popular. Men enjoy playing a card came called *baloot*. Women often visit other women at their homes or in cafés. Saudis also enjoy watching movies at home.

BALOOT

MAKE YOUR OWN CAMELS!

Arabian camels are beloved animals in Saudi Arabia. Make your own from homemade dough!

What You Need:
- a mixing bowl
- 4 cups all-purpose flour
- 1 cup salt
- 1 1/2 cups warm water
- acrylic or tempera paint
- paintbrushes
- glitter gel (optional)

Instructions:
1. Look at pictures to shape your camels.
2. Mix the flour, salt, and water until the dough is smooth.
3. Roll out the dough with a rolling pin or your hands and cut camel shapes from it.
4. Have an adult help you bake the camels in the oven at 300 degrees Fahrenheit (149 degrees Celsius) for one hour. Once they are hard, take them out of the oven and let them cool.
5. Use paint or glitter gel to decorate your camels.

FOOD

NO PORK ON THE MENU

As a Muslim country, Saudi Arabia forbids certain foods that Islam does not allow. Pork is never eaten or sold in the country.

Saudi Arabian food is very flavorful. Breakfasts may include flat bread with date jam or yogurt. A spicy egg dish called *shakshuka* can be enjoyed with Arabic coffee or mint tea.

Meat, fish, and rice are found in many main dishes. *Kabsa* is the national dish. It features meat, rice, and many spices. A stuffed lamb dish called *khuzi* is popular throughout the country. Grilled meat skewers with vegetables called *kebabs* are also a Saudi favorite. For dessert, Saudis enjoy fresh fruit and dried dates. They also eat small pastries or puddings such as *mahalabia*.

SHAKSHUKA

KABSA

KEBABS

MAHALABIA

This creamy pudding is easy to make and enjoy! Try preparing this dessert with the help of an adult.

Ingredients:

3 cups milk
3/4 cup white sugar
1 cup cold water
6 tablespoons of cornstarch
1 cup heavy whipping cream
1 tablespoon of rose water or 1/2 teaspoon vanilla extract
2 ground cardamom pods

Steps:
1. Combine the milk and sugar in a saucepan. Bring to a boil.
2. Mix the water and cornstarch together in a bowl until smooth. Stir into boiling milk.
3. Cook the milk mixture over medium heat for 15 to 20 minutes, until thick.
4. Remove the saucepan from the heat.
5. Stir the cream, rose water, and cardamom into the milk mixture.
6. Refrigerate the milk mixture for 2 to 3 hours until it is completely cooled. Then enjoy this creamy treat!

CELEBRATIONS

Islamic holidays are very important to Saudis. During the holy month of Ramadan, Saudi Muslims celebrate the birth of Islam. *Eid al-Fitr* is celebrated at the end of the month. Saudis feast with their families and exchange gifts.

Every summer, Muslims participate in *Eid al-Adha*. This time marks the end of the **pilgrimage** to Mecca. Families **sacrifice** an animal. They give equal parts of the meat to their families, neighbors, and those in need. Saudi National Day is celebrated on September 23. It celebrates the day that the kingdom was unified. Saudis celebrate their **culture** all year long!

EID AL-FITR
PERFORMANCE

THE PILGRIMAGE TO MECCA

Every year, millions of Muslims from around the world make the pilgrimage to Mecca. According to Islam, every believer who is physically and financially able to visit must go at least once during their lifetime.

1932
Abd al-Aziz officially forms the Kingdom of Saudi Arabia

1742
Sheikh Muhammad ibn 'Abd al-Wahhab and Muhammad ibn Saud work together to establish the first Saudi state as a place for the teaching of pure Islam

1938
Oil is discovered and manufactured under the U.S. controlled Aramco oil company

1818
Ottoman forces conquer Riyadh

1902
Abd al-Aziz takes back Riyadh

2015
Women run for office for the first time in Saudi Arabia and 20 get elected

1990
Saudi Arabia asks the U.S. and other nations to help keep Iraqi invaders out of the country during the Persian Gulf War

1980
Saudi Arabia buys the Aramco oil company from the U.S.

2011
Women are granted the right to vote and work in government

SAUDI ARABIA FACTS

Official Name: Kingdom of Saudi Arabia

Flag of Saudi Arabia: The Saudi Arabian flag is green, which is traditional in Islamic countries. It features large, white Arabic script that reads, "There is no god but God; Muhammad is the Messenger of God." A white, horizontal sword lies below the script.

Area: 830,000 square miles (2,149,690 square kilometers)

Capital City: Riyadh

Important Cities: Jeddah, Mecca, Medina, Dammam

Population: 34,173,498 (July 2020)

WHERE PEOPLE LIVE

COUNTRYSIDE **15.7%**

CITY **84.3%**

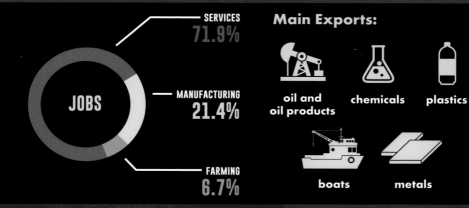

SERVICES
71.9%

Main Exports:

JOBS

MANUFACTURING
21.4%

oil and
oil products

chemicals

plastics

FARMING
6.7%

boats

metals

National Holiday:
Saudi National Day (September 23)

Main Language:
Arabic

Form of Government:
absolute monarchy

Title for Country Leader:
king

RELIGION

SUNNI
MUSLIM
90%

SHI'A
MUSLIM
10%

Unit of Money:
Saudi riyal

GLOSSARY

Arabic—related to people who are originally from the Arabian Peninsula and who now live mostly in the Middle East and northern Africa

culture—the beliefs, arts, and ways of life in a place or society

ethnic—related to a group of people who share customs and an identity

export—a product sold by one country to another

gulf—part of an ocean or sea that extends into land

Middle East—a region of southwestern Asia and northern Africa; this region includes Egypt, Lebanon, Iran, Iraq, Saudi Arabia, Syria, and other nearby countries.

native—originally from the area or related to a group of people that began in the area

nomadic—related to people who have no fixed home but wander from place to place

peninsula—a section of land that extends out from a larger piece of land and is almost completely surrounded by water

pilgrimage—a long journey to a holy place

plains—large areas of flat land

plateau—an area of flat, raised land

rural—related to the countryside

sacrifice—an offering of something valuable to please a god or gods

service jobs—jobs that perform tasks for people or businesses

tourism—the business of people traveling to visit other places

traditional—related to customs, ideas, or beliefs handed down from one generation to the next

urban—related to cities and city life

vocational—involved in the training of a skill or trade that prepares an individual for a career

TO LEARN MORE

AT THE LIBRARY

Klepeis, Alicia Z. *Iran*. Minneapolis, Minn.: Bellwether Media, 2020.

Oachs, Emily Rose. *Iraq*. Minneapolis, Minn.: Bellwether Media, 2018.

Sullivan, Laura L. *Saudi Arabia (Exploring World Cultures)*. New York, N.Y.: Cavendish Square, 2017.

ON THE WEB

FACTSURFER

Factsurfer.com gives you a safe, fun way to find more information.

1. Go to www.factsurfer.com.

2. Enter "Saudi Arabia" into the search box and click 🔍.

3. Select your book cover to see a list of related content.

INDEX

activities, 21
Albutairi, Fahad, 13
camels (craft), 21
capital (see Riyadh)
celebrations, 24-25
climate, 9
communities, 14-15
customs, 16-17
education, 18
Eid al-Adha, 24
Eid al-Fitr, 24
fast facts, 28-29
food, 22-23
housing, 14
Jeddah, 6, 14
landmarks, 4, 5
landscape, 8-9, 10, 14
language, 13
location, 6-7
Mecca, 6, 13, 24, 25
people, 12-13
Ramadan, 24
recipe, 23
religion, 13, 15, 16, 18,
   22, 24, 25

Riyadh, 4-5, 6, 7, 9, 14
Saudi National Day, 24
size, 7
sports, 20
timeline, 26-27
transportation, 14
wildlife, 10-11
work, 17, 19